ISBN 978-0-260-45372-3
PIBN 10949245

December 1945

U.S. DEPARTMENT OF AGRICULT

Production and Marketing Administratio

IN THIS ISSUE:

In December C. W. Kitchen, Assistant Administrator for Regulatory
and Marketing Service Work, PMA, made a speech at Washington. It
covered some of the chief problems in prospect for producers of agricultural products and the trade, and some of the things both industry
and Government can do about these problems. The bulk of that speech
is reproduced here.

The 1945 Irish potato crop was the third largest on record. Ample
supplies may provide some distribution problems in 1946. Here are some
things USDA is doing about potato distribution.

Consumers will welcome an early return of well-aged cheese, with
its firm body and clean, well-developed flavor, to replace the curdy or
rubbery product they had to take during the war years.

Address all inquiries to
Elbert O. Umsted
Editor, Marketing Activities
U. S. Department of Agriculture
Washington 25, D. C.

Material in Marketing Activities
may be reprinted without special
permission.

Issued monthly.   Vol. 8, No. 12

What's Ahead in Marketing?

In the marketing outlook for the next 12 months, perhaps the outstanding change from this past year will be the absence of most of the wartime regulations and controls--allocations, quotas and other restrictions, priorities, labor controls, and so on. Growers, shippers, handlers, processors, and other marketing agents will again be free to hire labor and to buy supplies and equipment as they please--provided they can locate the labor or the materials.

For the most part they should find the shortages that have plagued them during wartime pretty well cleared up. It will pay them to get orders in early for many items; and this will be a good thing anyway from the standpoint of providing manufacturers of containers, equipment, and other supplies a basis for going ahead full steam on reconversion.

More specifically, the prospect is that containers of various kinds, most other supplies, and facilities for processing and for storage should be adequate for 1946 needs. This includes cold storage, which...has been a problem during the war. Of course, if we should embark on a large-scale program of purchasing perishables to support prices and trying to hold them in storage instead of moving them into consumption, cold-storage facilities could get crowded very quickly. But as there was some expansion of space during the war, cooler and freezer facilities should be adequate to meet prospective normal needs of the trade.

The two spots where continuing serious bottlenecks are possible are in labor supply and transportation, especially refrigerated transportation. Everyone expects the labor market to be easier in the year ahead. The Office of War Mobilization and Reconversion estimates that there may be as many as 8 million unemployed next year. But this does not necessarily assure an easy labor supply for the food industries, or in the manufacture of containers and other supplies for to a large extent these are relatively low-wage industries. People who have been enjoying high wages in war industries will be slow to return 'to these lower-paid occupations. Liberal unemployment compensation will help them tide over while they are exploring fully the possibilities of finding jobs at the higher wage levels to which they have become accustomed. Thus the industries and trades associated with food handling and distribution will likely find themselves at the end of the line so far as easing of the labor shortage is concerned. While the situation will certainly be much better than it has been in the past few years, people in the food trades must not expect to find the labor market changing overnight.

On the transportation side, the end of military operations last summer was not followed by the sudden easing of all our transportation difficulties that some people had expected. The railroads are still having trouble handling all their traffic. This situation should continue to improve, however, and especially as more and more trucks become available again. But even in trucking, for a while the new equipment that becomes available will be used chiefly to replace worn-out trucks that have been kept on the road past their time.

The chief transportation bottleneck will be in refrigerated shipping. The number of refrigerator cars in service has declined during the war, falling from 146,000 in 1941 to less than 138,000 this year. The cars in use have seen very hard service in the last several years and many of them are in bad shape. The number out for heavy repairs increased by more than 2,000 during 1944 and the first half of 1945. The need for additional refrigerator cars is more pressing now than at any time during the war, and, so far, no really effective replacement program has gotten underway.

Two things will help to relieve this situation. The easing of the burden on railroad facilities generally will make possible more effective use of the available refrigerator cars. They will be less frequently tied up in yards and terminals or held back to let higher priority freight go through. And as motortrucks become more available there will be a shift back from rail to truck movement of perishables. The trend before the war was toward the use of motortrucks, and there is no indication at present that the railroads have any effective program planned to prevent the resumption of this trend.

There will, of course, be numerous marketing adjustment problems for individual commodities. There will be a reduced production of dehydrated vegetables and dried eggs, for example, and probably a shift back to a more normal pattern of milk utilization, and a need to find outlets for milk powder. There will be problems of price adjustments associated with the discontinuance of ceilings and subsidies. These will probably be discussed in commodity meetings....

Longer-Range Problems

Let us, turn to some of the longer-range marketing problems. The outstanding need over the next several years will be, as in the past, to achieve greater efficiency and lower cost, and to do a more effective job of merchandizing farm products.... We must do everything possible to get farm products to consumers at low mark-ups that will encourage consumption, and in the most attractive condition to stimulate demand. Government marketing services and other programs can supplement the efforts of producers and the trade, but the initiative will rest with the farmers, with the processors, and with the distributors themselves in developing and putting into practice better market methods.

To reduce marketing charges will not be easy. Margins for processing and handling many commodities have been held down during the war as part of the attempt to control the cost of living. Many processors and distributors have been squeezed. On a number of foods it has even been necessary to resort to Government subsidies to keep margins down and to hold the line on price ceilings. High costs and the shortage of labor have necessitated cutting out many services that are normally rendered; resumption of them will raise costs. Meanwhile, wages have gone up markedly, and the prospects are that they are going to stay up. The natural tendency of margins will be to widen.

Opportunities for Improvement

Let us turn briefly, therefore, to some of the opportunities that the present outlook offers for making marketing more efficient and doing a better merchandizing job on farm products. In the first place, wartime conditions have forced us to adopt many economies in marketing, and some of these may well be worth continuing. In the container field, for example, the need to get maximum output from manufacturing facilities and make most effective use of limited materials has brought about a lot more progress in standardization and simplification than we were able to accomplish in many years of talking, before the war. It would be unfortunate to give up the gains thus made.

There is currently a great deal of interest in the continuation of every-other-day delivery of milk. At the time this practice was being instituted there was considerable controversy as to whether it represented any real economy. Now, distributors seem generally agreed that return to daily delivery would require an increase in price to consumers. Regarding this and similar economy measures that cut down services rendered consumers, I would not advocate that they be made compulsory under peacetime conditions. I would insist, however, that as a means of widening the market for farm products the extra services should be charged for separately so that consumers who cannot afford to pay for them can still buy the product.

As transportation has been one of our serious problems during the war we have developed a great number of practices for conserving it. We have had pooling arrangements, the suspension of regulations that acted as barriers to interstate movement of commodities, economies of operation like heavier railroad car loadings. Not all of these wartime arrangements and practices will reflect real savings in peacetime when the burden on railroads eases and trucks become generally available. But some of them will, and we should take advantage of the lessons we have learned during the war.

Satisfactory transportation service at reasonable rates is basic to efficient marketing in an economic system such as ours where products move great distances to market. We should guard against rigidity of rate structures that thwart competitive testing of the relative efficiencies of different modes of transport. We should keep alive incentives for progressive new developments designed to reduce costs and improve the service rendered, and make sure that the economies achieved are properly reflected in rates. We should insist on equitable rates between areas so that the rate structure will not act as a barrier to desirable changes in distribution. During the last 5 years the Department has accomplished a great deal in effecting adjustments in rates for transporting farm products. Actions in which it has participated have saved nearly $650,000,000 in the total transportation bill.

Modernization

Special wartime conditions have given rise to a wide variety of improvements in methods of handling farm products—new methods of packaging, more efficient storage practices, the conversion of the northwest grain warehouses into elevators to permit the handling of grains in bulk rather than bags, processing improvements like assembly-line country eviscerating plants for poultry.

We now have an opportunity for wholesale modernization and improvement of facilities of all kinds. During the war the scarcity of labor and the shortage of materials prevented proper maintenance of many kinds of processing plants and other facilities. These plants now need overhauling. Meanwhile funds have accumulated in depreciation reserves. Now is the opportune time, therefore, for wholesale modernization and improvement of these plants and facilities. It is also a good time to consolidate inefficient plants that are no longer adapted to an economic scale of operation under present marketing conditions. Many small cooperative creameries are already considering consolidation with neighboring plants to get establishments of efficient size, with modern equipment, and with possibilities for diversified operation that will enable them to take much better advantage of varying relative returns for butter, cheese, powder, and other dairy products. There are similar opportunities in cotton ginning, in the development of country plants for assembling, grading, and packaging eggs and poultry, and in other commodities.

Market Facilities

In the construction and modernization of markets for perishables—both terminal markets and concentration markets—we can hope that real progress will be made within the next few years. Before the war we did a lot of talking about the need for modernizing markets. We made several studies. A few markets were built, but not many. Now, with the increasing urgency of improving the handling of perishable products, and with the inadequacies of present facilities made even more evident, there are signs that we are going to get real action. The number of State and local agencies that have come to the Department of Agriculture for consultation and advice on improving their market facilities has greatly increased. Many of these States and communities are formulating definite plans and developing financial arrangements to carry them through. The desirability of improved modern markets as public-works projects has been recognized, and funds for constructing them are going to be made available in any general public-works program that goes into action.

This and many of the other developments touched upon are going to provide an opportunity for doing a better merchandizing job on farm products. They will facilitate better grading, handling, and packaging. They will make distribution more efficient and less costly—thus promoting simultaneously better returns to producers and more attractive prices to consumers. They will help in maintaining the quality of farm products during their movement from producer to consumer, and contribute in other ways to getting them into the retail store in more convenient and more attractive form.

On the merchandizing side, we shall need to be alert to possibilities of developing new outlets and exploiting old markets more effectively. In the fruit and vegetable field, for example, there is a well-recognized opportunity for better exploitation of the smaller consuming centers. Shipments, especially of perishables, have been too largely directed to the larger markets capable of absorbing daily carlot shipments. Supplies going to the smaller markets have been spotty and intermittent. Refrigerated truck transportation and other improved handling methods provide a real opportunity for progressive distributors to open up these smaller markets and develop a profitable business in them.

Another merchandizing opportunity grows out of the wartime emphasis on nutritional education. American consumers are much more conscious than they were 4 years ago of the importance to health of eating the right foods—getting their vitamins, minerals, and the like. They are also much better informed on what foods make up a proper diet. The food trades can perform a real service, as well as promote their own businesses, by helping to spread this nutritional education work and by following through on it to supply the potential demand that it creates. They carry their word to consumers at the point of consumption—an outstanding advantage in translating nutritional principles into day-to-day shopping habits. Many of our "problem" commodities can be promoted through the nutritional appeal.

Government Cooperation

So far we have been considering mostly the responsibilities of producers and the trade, and what they can do to improve the post-war marketing of farm products. What is the role of Government services and marketing activities in this development? The Government stands ready to assist producers and the trade through service programs, research, and education. It can cooperate in surveying and analyzing problems. It can provide a clearing house of information. It can consult and advise, and can sponsor and help group efforts to work out programs in the public interest.

More specifically, there is clear need for improving the existing marketing services when adapting them to post-war conditions. Orderly marketing requires widening the market news service to cover more markets. Market information is needed regarding smaller consuming centers to aid the attempt to exploit them more effectively. It should provide data on more commodities--for example, processed fruits and vegetables. It should cover more stages of marketing--for example, current information on retail prices. More data should be available periodically on costs and charges at all stages of marketing, as an indication where the most promising economies lie, and as a measure of progress in achieving them. Information on supplies and prices should be more widely disseminated and there is particular opportunity for closer cooperation with States and local communities in getting advice on the relative abundance of foods directly to the housewives themselves.

Similarly with the grading and inspection service, there is need for wider coverage, especially in receiving markets. There is need to improve standards for many commodities to make them more widely useful in the trade. And there is need to widen the dissemination of grade information--particularly for greater extension of it to the consumer level where the housewives can rely upon it as a guide in their purchases.

Steps to be Taken

These, in brief, seem to be some of the chief problems in marketing over the next several years and some of the chief opportunities for marketing improvements to meet these problems. How can we organize for action to take advantage of these opportunities?

In the first place, old-fashioned competition will provide the spur and the test of many trade efforts. A chief function of Government continues to be the fostering of competition and the maintenance of a framework, through services and regulatory activities, within which it can function. Alert, progressive producers and tradesmen who have ingenuity and initiative will continue to demonstrate the effectiveness of the competitive system in providing an economical marketing system.

But the achievement of many marketing improvements requires cooperative action. On the producers' side this means expanding the role of marketing cooperatives as organizations to help growers prepare and sell their products more effectively and to assure them fair returns.

Marketing Agreements

There is need to expand the role of marketing agreements. The inadequacies of the present Marketing Agreement Act are widely recognized and there has been widespread discussion of needed amendments. A particular difficulty that came up during the war was the necessity of suspending agreements whenever prices went above parity. Prices are now generally above parity but there is the prospect that they will go down. We need

Marketing Activities

to be able to take steps to protect the orderly operation of markets
in advance of this price decline, rather than wait for the bottom to
drop out of the market and chaos to develop before any action is started.

Then we can envision a much wider role for the marketing agreement
technique than it has had in the past. It seems...to offer excellent
possibilities for Government and industry cooperation in achieving many
of the improvements in marketing organization and practice that we have
been discussing. With adequate safeguards to consumers against abuse,
marketing agreements and orders provide a means for instituting practices
that are generally agreed upon as desirable but that cannot be put into
operation without protection against chiseling minorities.

Regional and Commodity Programs

Interstate cooperation in the development of marketing programs
is another type of action that needs to be more widely adopted.
Organizations like the Council of State Governments and the New England
Research Council have done outstanding work on ways to improve marketing.
The short-time research project on agricultural and economic problems
of the Cotton Belt, now getting underway, exemplifies the possibility
for cooperation of trade and industry, State College people, and
Federal Government agencies in the development of integrated regional
and commodity programs.

Better integration of production and marketing plans is a need
that we have come to recognize during the war. We are currently con-
fronted, for example, with a marketing problem arising from beef-cattle
herd improvement in the Southeast. This area has made outstanding
progress in developing and improving its herds for economic production
of good-quality beef, but there has been no simultaneous development
of market outlets for this production or of market facilities for
handling it. The two developments should have gone hand in hand.

During the war, under the goals programs, we have made real
progress--though with many faltering steps--in integrating our production
and marketing programs. We have learned to develop production goals
in terms of national requirements for farm products. We have learned to
examine goals and to adjust them in the light of the availability of
transportation, storage, packaging materials, processing facilities, and
other marketing resources. We have learned to plan marketing programs
that will go hand in hand with production programs, so that the foods
and fibers produced on the farm can be distributed in orderly fashion.
We must take advantage of this experience to continue, in both our
shorter-range and our longer-range planning, more effective integration
of production and marketing programs than we had before the war.

Finally, we cannot emphasize too much...the importance of educational work as a means of bringing marketing improvements into actual
practice--of enabling us to market as well as we know how. Much of the

responsibility must rest on producers and the trade for doing the kind of marketing job that will make possible the maintenance of satisfactory incomes and prices to producers. Producers themselves must learn how to sort, pack, and sell their products so as to get the full benefit of the quality they have produced. They must take care of the eggs so they will reach the market with the highest proportion of Grade A's. And handlers all along the line, from the country dealer on, must learn and equip themselves to preserve the quality of the goods they receive from farmers--to keep the eggs in Grade A condition until they reach consumers. They must learn to organize their operations efficiently and to take advantage of practices that will keep their costs down.

Government research is worthless except as it is translated into actual practice through educational work with producers and trade groups. Government services and regulatory activities--market news and grading-- might as well be discontinued except as producers and dealers and ultimate consumers know about them and take advantage of them.

Education, cooperation, and competition--these are three slow and painstaking methods of bringing about improvement. But they are the methods that we rely on in our society because we believe they are conducive to the surest and most permanent results in the end, and because they pre- serve freedom and initiative along the way.

- -

COTTON INSULATION PROGRAM ANNOUNCED

A program to promote the use of cotton in the manufacture of insu- lating materials through June 30, 1947, was announced December 20 by the Department of Agriculture.

Insulation manufacturers currently participating in a Department program are receiving a Government payment of 9 cents a pound on the batt part of finished insulation (excluding backing material and metal fasteners), and have through March 30, 1946, to complete their opera- tions.

The announcement provided for Government payment of 9 cents per pound on insulation manufactured through June 30, 1946, unless OPA ceiling prices were increased or suspended before July 1, 1946.

If the OPA ceiling prices were increased or suspended, the Govern- ment payment was to be reduced to 7½ cents per pound for the day following the effective date of increase or suspension to June 30, 1946.

From July 1, 1946, through June 30, 1947, the rate of payment will be 7½ cents per pound, whether or not there are OPA ceilings. This payment will be made on insulation composed of not less than 50 percent (by weight) of lint cotton not shorter than 3/4 inch in staple and not lower in grade than the lowest grade in the Universal Standards for American Upland cotton.

Manufacturers wishing to participate in the revised program should file applications with the Cotton Branch, Production and Marketing Administration, U. S. Department of Agriculture, Washington 25, D. C.

FOREIGN COTTON STORAGE ORDER TERMINATED

Termination of WFO 117, as amended, controlling the storage of foreign cotton entering the United States in bond for later transhipment to other countries, was announced early in December by the Department of Agriculture.

This order was issued October 17, 1944, to make storage space available for 750,000 bales of 1944-crop Texas, Oklahoma, and other Western-grown cotton that had been stored on the ground.

The order was no longer needed because adequate storage had become available for all American cotton. The 1945 crop was smaller than the 1944 crop, and considerable space had been made available as a result of increased cotton exports and releases of space by Government agencies which had been storing war materials in cotton warehouses.

RESTRICTIONS ON BREWERS' USE
OF MALTED GRAIN LIBERALIZED

USDA has increased by 20 percent the amount of malt which brewers may use in the 3-month quota period commencing December 1, 1945. The action was taken through an amendment to WFO 66, which controls brewers' purchases and use of malted grain, hops, and rice.

Before the action, brewers were limited to 93 percent of base-year use in each quota period if 93 percent of their malted grain use in the base year exceeded 70,000 bushels. They were limited to 100 percent of the amount used in the base year if 93 percent of their malted grain use in the base year was 70,000 bushels or less. Any brewer who operated in the base year could use at least 3,000 bushels of malted grain in any quota period.

Liberalization of malt usage was made possible because of an increase in the supply of malt resulting from reduced requirements for industrial alcohol since the end of the war.

Irish Potato Review

In 1945, American farmers planted 2,846,000 acres of Irish potatoes and produced a 425,131,000-bushel crop, the third largest on record and 11 percent larger than the crop of 1944. The 1945 crop in the 30 late States is expected to total 329 million bushels, and in the 18 surplus late States which provide the major storage stocks for commercial shipment during late fall, winter, and early spring a 297-million-bushel crop is indicated. Maine alone had a crop of 53 million bushels and Idaho, coming in second, had 44 million bushels. The 7 "intermediate" States hung up a record of 41 percent more potatoes than last year's short crop.

The yield per acre was 8 percent higher than the highest on record, principally the result of increased plantings in high-producing commercial States. Without the higher-than-average yield per acre the crop would have been about 7 percent smaller than an average crop. In addition to the commercial crop, homegrown potatoes from backyard plots were consumed locally and amateur gardeners sold small quantities of potatoes in nearby markets.

Last year, United States civilians consumed 126 pounds of potatoes apiece. This year the per capita consumption of potatoes is expected to reach 130 pounds. Potato supplies probably will average substantially the same next year as in 1945. The 1944 crop had been the second largest in 10 years. In addition we imported about 9 million bushels from Canada.

Supplies Ample

The bumper crop of late potatoes assures ample supplies for this winter and next spring. A large carry-over of these is expected. This, plus next year's crop, may be enough to cause some distribution problems, particularly in view of reduced military requirements and the possible dwindling of civilian demand. Potatoes will be plentiful through the first half of 1946.

Fortunately, not all of the potato crop comes to harvest at the same time. But early and intermediate varieties do not keep well and must be moved quickly into consumer channels. The late variety will keep over the winter without refrigeration. Most of the early crop was harvested by mid-July in 12 States. California contributed about 37 percent or 24 million bushels of early potatoes. Movement of potatoes became freer when the Department of Agriculture terminated War Food Order 120 on August 29, 1945. The order, effective since December 1944, had assured the procurement of good quality potatoes for the armed forces and other Government agencies and prevented the diversion of seed potatoes from planting areas. It was terminated because supplies had become more than enough to meet anticipated Government requirements.

Marketing Activities

Military demand and transportation difficulties resulted in a shortage in civilian potato supplies in some areas last year. Present and prospective stocks are generous, but to move them into many civilian markets at prevailing prices may prove difficult. In addition, transportation problems have increased because of a car shortage which is more acute now than during the war.

Surplus Stocks

In contrast with last year, when we imported 9 million bushels of potatoes (mostly table stock) from Canada, during the year ending next June 30, United States imports probably will amount to less than 2 million bushels, almost entirely seed stock. Canada has a short crop and has arranged to take 4½ million bushels of our potatoes. Since the total of our support price and freight charges is greater than Canada's price ceiling, the difference is subsidized by the Canadian Government under an agreement between the two countries.

With 45 million bushels of potatoes more than we need for civilian consumption, the Government has planned loan, purchase, and diversion programs to support prices. Under the purchase program it has diverted 11,470 carloads of potatoes during the last 5 months. These potatoes included quantities for starch and industrial alcohol manufacture, relief programs, stock feed, canning, and sale.

Exports to Europe will take up some more of the slack and provide much-needed food for war-ravaged countries. Belgium will receive 1 million bushels of late potatoes which the Government bought from certified dealers and growers at support prices. The French Government is buying 4½ million bushels, originally purchased by USDA at support levels, at prices somewhat below support levels.

Prices dropped from ceiling to support levels in midsummer. Prices to farmers dropped from $1.83 a bushel in July to $1.26 in October. In view of the reduction in military needs, the availability of other foods, the possible decrease in employment and consumer income, and the likelihood that the high acreages of recent years will be maintained, growers' prices are not likely to go much above support-price levels for the 1945 potato crop marketing season. But these prices are about twice those of most pre-war years.

Outlook

The high prices that farmers received for potatoes during this and three preceding seasons and support prices at not less than 90 percent of parity make it likely that farmers will plant about the same acreage to potatoes in 1946 as during the last two seasons. The downward trend in potato acreage during the last 10 years is offset by an acreage expansion in high-producing commercial States which probably will continue in 1946, with prospects of a crop of from 380 to 400 million bushels. If production should reach 400 million bushels, prices above minimum support levels are unlikely and a surplus disposal problem may result.

The 1946 crop of early potatoes to be marketed next winter and spring will compete with 1945-crop late potatoes at a figure reflecting support-price levels. A crop of early potatoes as large in 1945 as in the past 3 years may mean temporary oversupplies and require the operation of support-price and surplus-disposal programs.

The Price-Support Program

With a price-supporting program on potatoes, farmers have not been traveling entirely at their own risk. There is assurance of support at not less than 90 percent of parity--which means a national average of about $1.10 to $1.15 per bushel. From October 1 to December 10, 1945, the Government made loans on 319,661 bushels of potatoes. The 1946 price-support program will differ in two respects from that of previous years. There will be no advance announcement of support prices for grades below U. S. No. 1 at fixed amounts or at fixed percentages of the applicable prices for U. S. No. 1 grade. The Department of Agriculture will support prices of lower grades, exclusive of culls, "at such times, in such areas, by such means, and at such prices" as are necessary in order to fulfill price-support objectives. The Department may specify conditions under which grades lower than U. S. No. 1 may be disposed of before No. 1 grade potatoes would be eligible for support.

Support prices announced are base prices for potatoes "in bulk, loaded on truck at farmer's gate" instead of on an f. o. b. basis. The price a participating farmer receives will be the base price plus marketing service which he is directed to perform. The Government will purchase early and intermediate crop potatoes and if necessary divert them to other than normal trade channels, including export, industrial, and feed outlets. Loans will support late-crop potato prices with diversion--where necessary and feasible--to export, industrial, and feed outlets.

The price-support program for potatoes became active in August when prices of intermediate potatoes dropped from ceiling to support levels because of the overloaded market. In the fall, when growers' prices fell below late-crop support levels at some shipping points, the Government again brought diversion and loan programs into play. Purchases included New Jersey and Long Island potatoes not suitable for extended storage periods.

To utilize surplus stocks of intermediate-crop eastern potatoes, a large Philadelphia plant received potatoes at the rate of 75 cars daily for the manufacture of butyl alcohol used in paints, lacquers, and synthetic rubber. An ethyl alcohol plant at Muscatine, Iowa, is using surplus potatoes for the production of motor fuel and antifreeze solutions. A second plant at Omaha, Nebr., was expected to carry on similar operations. Now both plants are planning a shift to glucose production to assist in meeting the need for sweetener products.

Except for the diversion of potatoes for industrial products (principally starch in Maine), loans are expected to be the only potato price-support means active for the rest of this season. No increase over the December price support for 1945 late-crop Irish potatoes is expected for the remainder of the marketing season ending in June 1946.

CORN LOAN RATES FOR 1945 CROP ANNOUNCED

Corn loan rates for the 1945 crop, ranging by counties from 90 cents to $1.13 per bushel and averaging $1.01 nationally, were announced in mid-December by the U. S. Department of Agriculture. Last year's national average was 98 cents a bushel, the rates by counties varying from 87 cents to $1.10.

The 1945 rates are based upon 90 percent of the parity price of corn as of October 1, 1945. Parity on that date was $1.12 as a national average, as contrasted with $1.09 at the same time last year.

Corn eligible for loans must grade No. 3 or better, except for moisture content, or No. 4 on test weight only. Corn grading "mixed" will have a loan value of 2 cents a bushel less.

Loans will be available to producers from December 1, 1945, through May 31, 1946. The loans will be evidenced by notes maturing on demand but not later than September 1, 1946.

Corn producers' notes will bear interest at the rate of 3 percent per annum, and will be secured by chattel mortgages. Producers may pay off the loans at any time prior to September 1, 1946, or they may voluntarily deliver the collateral in satisfaction of loans on and after that date.

Upon delivery of corn grading higher than No. 3, the producer will be credited with a premium of $\frac{1}{2}$ cent per bushel for No. 2 and 1 cent per bushel for No. 1 above the applicable loan rate.

FIRE-CURED AND DARK AIR-CURED
TOBACCO GROWERS VOTE MARKETING QUOTAS

Official returns of the fire-cured and dark air-cured tobacco marketing quota referenda, held October 20, were released early in December.

Of the 13,557 farmers voting in the fire-cured tobacco referendum, 12,313 (90.8 percent) favored quotas for the three marketing years beginning October 1, 1946. Quotas were opposed by 866 farmers (or 6.4 percent of the total), and 378 votes (2.8 percent) were cast for quotas for a 1-year period.

Of the 18,167 farmers voting in the dark air-cured referendum, 17,464 (96.1 percent) favored quotas for the three marketing years beginning October 1, 1946. Quotas were opposed by 438 farmers (2.4 percent of the total) and 265 votes (1.5 percent) were cast for quotas for a 1-year period.

Any farmer who, as a landlord, tenant, or sharecropper, had an interest in the 1945 crop of these kinds of tobacco was eligible to vote in the referenda. Approximately 55 percent of the eligible producers voted in the fire-cured referendum and approximately 67 percent of the eligible producers voted in the dark air-cured referendum.

As more than two-thirds of those voting favored quotas, marketing quotas will be in effect on fire-cured and dark air-cured tobacco for the three marketing years beginning October 1, 1946.

COFFEE IMPORT CONTROLS SUSPENDED

Raw, green, roasted, or processed coffee has been removed from the list of imported items controlled by WFO 63, the Department of Agriculture has announced. Effective November 19, 1945, the action was in line with the recent announcements and a directive from the Office of War Mobilization and Reconversion relative to payment of a subsidy to importers of green coffee who meet the eligibility requirements of the directive. Control of coffee imports was to be suspended for the duration of the subsidy program to facilitate movement of coffee into this country in the period ending March 31, 1946.

FATS AND OILS ORDER AMENDED

The U. S. Department of Agriculture has amended WFO 42 to include the definitions for edible fats and oils products formerly contained within Ration Order 16, recently terminated by the Office of Price Administration. The amendment (No. 23) to WFO 42 does not change the order operation in any way. It merely continues the same definitions as existed during the rationing period because these products, controlled by WFO 42, were defined through direct reference to RO 16. The amendment became effective December 17, 1945.

Cheese Curing Time Halved

Manufacturers of American Cheddar cheese can now produce "aged cheese" of excellent quality and flavor in about 3 to 4 months—half the time formerly required. The new faster-curing method, developed by research workers in the Bureau of Dairy Industry, is entirely feasible under commercial conditions. It is also simple and economical.

Consumers will welcome an early return of well-aged cheese, with its firm body and clean, well-developed flavor, to replace the curdy or rubbery product they had to take during the war years. Supply and demand conditions during the war were such that little or no cheese was held for aging.

The Bureau found that cheese held in the curing room at 60 degrees Fahrenheit was as fully ripened in 3 to 4 months as cheese held at 50 degrees or lower for 6 to 8 months, provided the cheese was made from good-quality milk that had been pasteurized. The cheese held at the higher temperature also developed more and better flavor than the cheese held at the lower temperatures.

Pasteurization Important

The method is an outgrowth of earlier Bureau work which demonstrated that the use of pasteurized milk was an important step in producing cheese that would be uniformly high in quality. Pasteurization was adopted by many cheese makers during the war years.

To produce uniformly high-quality cheese, the Bureau advocates the use of milk of good quality, pasteurization of the milk, and the use of good starters. It has developed a reliable method for making the cheese, in which a controlled time schedule maintains the acidity within proper limits during the manufacturing process.

Pasteurization of the milk eliminates most of the undesirable factors, including disease-producing microorganisms, and the time-schedule method produces a relatively dry cheese that can be ripened safely and rapidly at the higher temperatures.

Bureau specialists believe their experimental results are sufficiently convincing to overcome the notion of many cheese makers that cheese made from pasteurized milk cannot be ripened fast enough and that it does not have enough of the characteristic Cheddar flavor. The specialists emphasize, however, that the higher curing temperature (up to 60 degrees F.) can be used safely only when the cheese is made from milk that is of good quality and that has been completely pasteurized.

USDA TERMINATES WFO 74

WFO 74, which permitted licensed ship suppliers to obtain set-aside
and restricted foods for War Shipping Administration vessels, was terminated effective December 1, 1945. The action was taken because War
Food orders affecting many of the foods covered under WFO 74 have been
suspended or terminated. As a result, the need of ship suppliers for
the procurement assistance provided by the order has diminished to
the point that the continuance of WFO 74 is no longer considered
necessary.

WFO 74 (formerly known as Food Distribution Regulation No. 3) was
put into effect December 1, 1943. By means of a certificate plan, ship
suppliers holding licenses under the order were enabled to purchase
and stockpile set-aside and restricted foods for ultimate delivery to
ships operating under the direction of the War Shipping Administration
and vessels of allied or neutral countries named by that agency. These
foods were used to feed ships' crews, Navy armed guards, Navy gun crews,
and troops carried on War Shipping Administration troop transports.
WFO 74 also gave the Department of Agriculture effective control over
scarce foods required by ships for ship stores, eliminated the cumber-
some process of direct procurement by War Shipping Administration, and
permitted the ship supply business to remain in the hands of commercial
suppliers.

HIGH-TEST MOLASSES INTO SIRUPS FOR CIVILIAN USE

Prospective sale by USDA of 12,600,000 gallons of high-test or
invert molasses, to be reprocessed for civilian food use, was announced
on December 20. The molasses, located at Port Everglades, Fla., was
originally acquired by the Defense Supplies Corporation to make industrial alcohol for the synthetic rubber and munitions programs.

Greatly reduced needs of these programs and short sugar supplies
made it possible and desirable to divert this high-test molasses to the
manufacture of sirups for human food use.

Department plans were to sell the molasses to processors who could
convert it into fine table sirups and sirups to be used in the manufacture of food products. Sales were to be restricted to outlets which
secure authorizations from the Department under the provisions of WFO 51.
This order controls the use and delivery of edible molasses.

Prospective purchasers who can use a minimum of a tank car load of
this molasses may obtain permits to sample it at Port Everglades, Fla.,
by applying to the Sugar Branch, U. S. Department of Agriculture,
Washington 25, D. C.

ABOUT MARKETING:

The following addresses and publications, issued recently, may be obtained upon request. To order, check on this page the publications desired, detach, and mail to the Production and Marketing Administration, U. S. Department of Agriculture, Washington 25, D. C.

Addresses:

Time to Look Ahead, by Clinton P. Anderson, Secretary of Agriculture, at Washington, D. C. December 5, 1945. 15 pp. (Mimeographed.)

A Look Ahead, by J. B. Hutson, Under Secretary of Agriculture and Administrator of the Production and Marketing Administration, at Columbus, Ohio. December 20, 1945. 13 pp. (Mimeographed.)

Publications:

Domestic Cotton Surplus Disposal Programs. MP 577. (United States Department of Agriculture) September 1945. 51 pp. (Printed.)

Standard-Density Cotton-Gin Presses. Circular No. 733. August 1945. 16 pp. (Printed.)

Directory of the Meat Inspection Division. July 1945. 44 pp. (Printed.)

1946 Agricultural Outlook Charts. (Bureau of Agricultural Economics) December 1945. 111 pp. (Multilithed.)

Regulations and Instructions Governing Origin Verification of Alfalfa and Red Clover Seed. September 1945. 26 pp. (Mimeographed.)

Citrus Fruits—Production, Farm Disposition, Value and Utilization of Sales, Crop Seasons, 1909-10--1943-44. (Bureau of Agricultural Economics) October 1945. 44 pp. (Mimeographed.)

Citrus: Revised Estimates of Production and Utilization, 1943-44 and 1944-45. (Bureau of Agricultural Economics) October 1945. 5 pp. (Mimeographed.)

Farm Production, Farm Disposition, and Value of Cotton and Cottonseed, and Related Data, 1928-44, by States. (Bureau of Agricultural Economics) October 1945. 41 pp. (Mimeographed.)

Monthly Sales of Principal Field Crops, 1944 Crop, by Leading Marketing States and for the United States with Comparisons. (Bureau of Agricultural Economics) November 1945. 13 pp. (Mimeographed.)

U. S. Standards for Fresh Shelled Lima Beans for Processing. (Effective December 27, 1945) 2 pp. (Mimeographed.)

Lightning Source UK Ltd.
Milton Keynes UK
UKHW020758270219

338009UK00008B/1760/P